THE
NARRAGANSETT

by Craig A. Doherty and Katherine M. Doherty

Illustrated by Richard Smolinski

ROURKE PUBLICATIONS, INC.

VERO BEACH, FLORIDA 32964

CONTENTS

Library of Congress Cataloging-in-Publication Data

Doherty, Craig A.
  The Narragansett / by Craig A. Doherty, Katherine M. Doherty.
    p. cm. — (Native American people)
  Includes bibliographical references.
    1. Narragansett Indians—Juvenile literature. [1. Narragansett Indians. 2. Indians of North America.] I. Doherty, Katherine M. II Title. III. Series.
E99.N16D64 1994   974'.004973—dc20   93-32669
  ISBN 0-86625-525-7   CIP
                             AC

Introduction

For many years, archaeologists—and other people who study early Native American cultures—agreed that the first humans to live in the Americas arrived about 11,500 years ago. These first Americans were believed to have been big-game hunters who lived by hunting the woolly mammoths and giant bison that inhabited the Ice Age plains of the Americas. This widely accepted theory also asserted that these first Americans crossed a land bridge linking Siberia, in Asia, to Alaska. This land bridge occurred when the accumulation of water in Ice Age glaciers lowered the level of the world's oceans.

In recent years, many scientists have challenged this theory. Although most agree that many big-game hunting bands left similar artifacts all over the Americas 11,500 years ago, many now suggest that the first Americans may have arrived as far back as 20,000 or even 50,000 years ago. There are those who think that some of these earliest Americans may have even come to the Americas by boat, working their way down the west coast of North America and South America.

In support of this theory, scientists who study either language or genetics (the study of the inherited similarities and differences found in living things) believe that there may have been more than one period of migration. They

also believe that these multiple migrations started in different parts of Asia, which accounts for the genetic and language differences among the people of the Americas. Although it is still not certain when the first Americans arrived, scientists agree that today's Native Americans are descendants of early Asian immigrants.

Over the thousands of years between the first arrivals from Asia and the introduction of Europeans, the people living in the Americas flourished and inhabited every corner of the two continents. Native Americans lived above the Arctic Circle in the North to Tierra del Fuego at the tip of South America, and from the Atlantic Ocean in the East to the Pacific Ocean in the West.

During this time, the people of North America divided into hundreds of different groups. Each group adapted to the environment in which it lived. As agriculture developed and spread throughout the Americas, some people switched from being nomads to living in one area. In the Southwest, along the Mississippi River, in Mexico, and in Peru, different groups of Native Americans built large cities. In other areas, groups continued to exist as hunters and gatherers who had no permanent settlements.

In what is now the eastern United States and Canada, Native Americans developed what is called Woodland culture. Many tribes shared this Woodland culture, which gets its name from the dependence of these people on the forests that surrounded them. The Narragansett tribe, which was primarily located in what is now the state of Rhode Island, is one example of a Woodland tribe.

Origins of the Narragansett

Over the thousands of years that scientists know that people have been in the northeastern section of North America, there has been a drastic, yet slow, shift in climate. At one point, glaciers covered what is now New England. As the Ice Age came to an end, large herds of Ice Age mammals roamed the area. People survived by hunting these animals. As the climate became more moderate, the large animals began to disappear, and people of the area adjusted their lifestyles.

Small bands of Native Americans expanded in the Northeast. They learned to hunt smaller animals and utilize the wide variety of edible wild plants that grew there. The bands that ranged along the coast learned how to harvest the tidal waters of the Atlantic. Approximately 2,500 years ago, the practices of agriculture first appeared in the Northeast. Corn was the major staple of Native American agriculture and had been first developed from a wild plant by the Native Americans in Mexico and Central America.

The introduction of agriculture allowed the various groups of the Northeast to settle in semipermanent villages. Although Native Americans did not privately own land, each group had a clearly defined territory. Usually the different groups within an area spoke a dialect, which is a slightly different version of the same language. The Narragansett spoke a dialect of the Algonquian language. This language was spoken by the Native Americans of the Atlantic coastal plain from what is now the Canadian Maritime Provinces

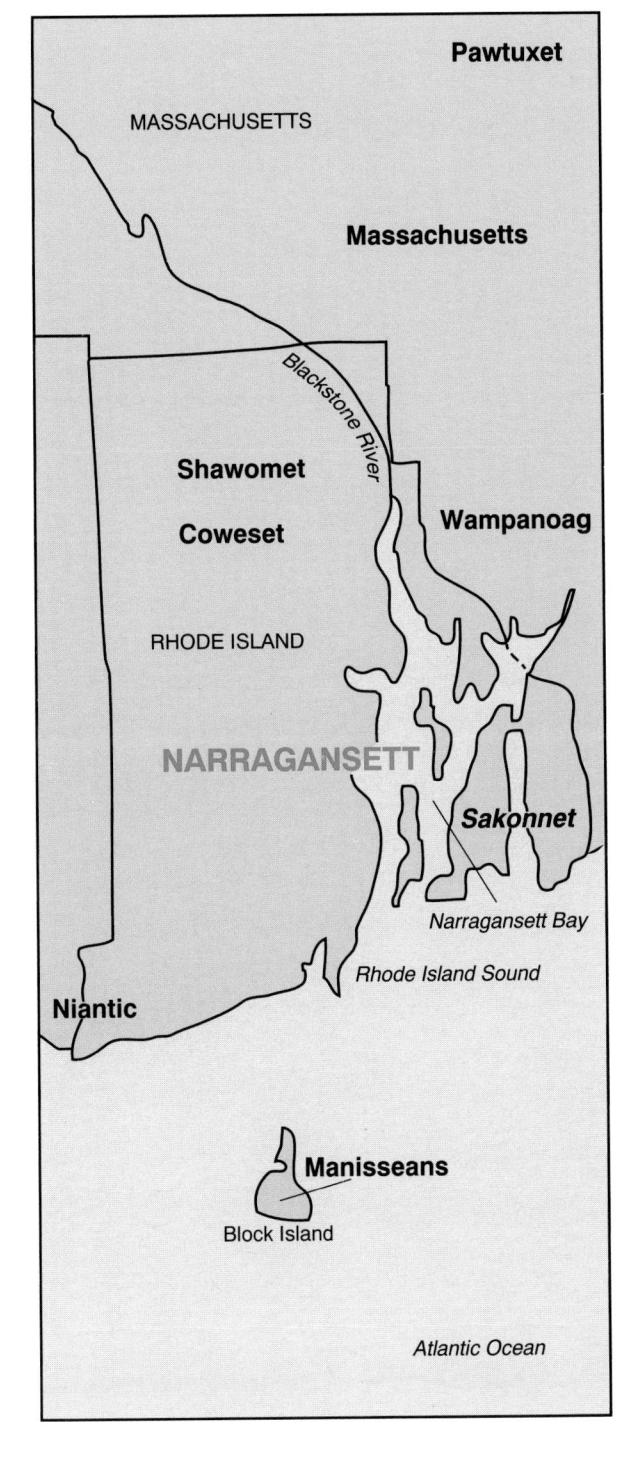

The Narragansett settled around a bay in what is now the state of Rhode Island. Europeans later named this bay after the tribe.

Daily Life

By the sixteenth century, before the Europeans had arrived, the Narragansett and other Woodland tribes had become highly organized farmers who supplemented their diets with wild plants, game, and fish. A Narragansett village typically had three to twenty-four dwellings. The villages of the Narragansett were semipermanent, depending on the quality of the soil at a particular site. When the soil near the village became worn out and their crops didn't produce enough food, the Narragansett would move to a new location within their territory.

The size and shape of Narragansett houses varied, depending upon use and the time of year. During the warmer months, most families lived in a *wigwam* that was fourteen to sixteen feet in diameter. A Narragansett *wigwam* was made by burying the ends of flexible poles around a circle in the earth and then bending them over and tying them together to make a dome. Lighter poles were then lashed horizontally to the frame in order to give it strength. Finally, a covering was attached to the horizontal poles.

The Narragansett used two types of covering for their *wigwams*—large sheets of bark from birch and/or chestnut trees, and woven mats. The mats were made of leaves of bulrushes, which are also called cat-o'-nine-tails. The leaves were woven together and then sewn using fine, long strips of

to North Carolina. The Narragansett were able to communicate with other Algonquian-speaking tribes that lived near their territory. But the farther they traveled away from their home territory, the harder it was to understand the dialect spoken.

Wigwams *were used during the warmer months of the year.*

bark and a needle made from the rib bone of a deer. A hole was left in the *wigwam* roof to allow smoke from the fire to escape.

Inside the *wigwam,* the walls were often decorated with woven mats that had been dyed to form patterns. These mats were called *munnotaubana.* Narragansett beds, made of mats covered with the skins of wild animals, were often placed on sleeping platforms that were twelve to eighteen inches high. In the center of the *wigwam* was the cooking fire. Upright forked sticks were set up on opposite sides of the fire, and a stick was laid across and above the fire, from which cooking pots could hang.

In the winter, the Narragansett built a different-shaped structure, using the same basic technique. The winter homes of the Narragansett were as wide as thirty feet and as long as one hundred feet. These winter houses held as many as forty to fifty people, and had a long row of fires down the middle of the structure. The sleeping platforms were constructed along the walls. The mats from the summer houses were used again in the construction of the winter houses, but the poles and bark covering were replaced. The purpose of the winter houses was to concentrate resources and people in one structure for greater warmth and comfort.

Family Life

It is believed that Narragansett families were arranged in matriarchal fashion. (When a couple marries in matriarchal families, the husband becomes part of the wife's family.) An extended family group, made up of grandparents, parents, aunts, uncles, and children, worked together to provide enough food, clothing, and shelter for all of its members. Narragansett men normally had only one wife, although there were some exceptions.

Large winter homes enabled the Narragansett to gather under one roof and share their resources.

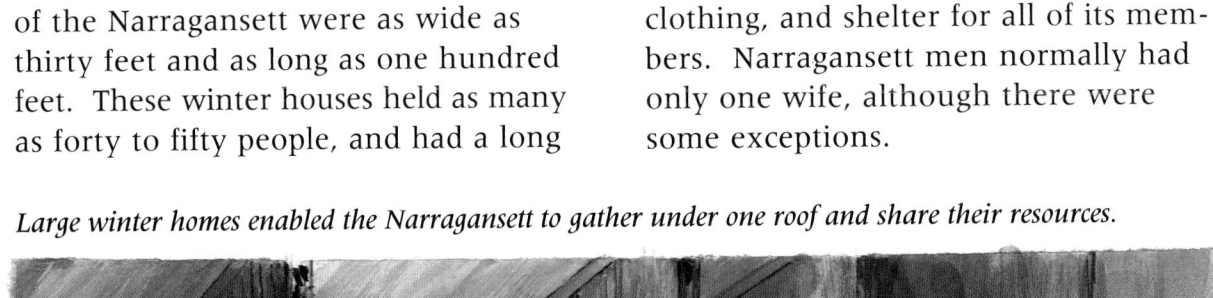

Raising children in a Narragansett family was a shared responsibility. When very young, the children were strapped to cradle boards. A mother carried her baby on a cradle board from place to place as she worked. The cradle board was set down or hung up when the mother needed her hands free to work. As soon as the children were able, they helped in the daily chores that needed to be done.

The children of the Narragansett were also given plenty of time to play. Archaeologists excavating Narragansett villages have found deerskin dolls decorated with beads. They have also found tops made of wood, bone, stone, and clay, as well as snow snakes. A snow snake is a stick that is about six to ten feet long and has been polished smooth. It is then slid along a frozen track, or on the ice. The point of this game was to see whose stick would slide the longest distance.

Children were instructed in the history and beliefs of the tribe by listening to stories, often while sitting around a fire. Storytelling was a frequent activity in the winter, when there was less to do. A good storyteller has always been a valued member of a tribe.

Food

Although corn was the primary staple of the Narragansett, their diet was varied and included a variety of foods. From the forest, the Narragansett gathered hazelnuts, hickory nuts, acorns, and walnuts. They also harvested the tubers (the fleshy parts of underground stems) that grew in the roots of the

A woman carries her child in a cradle board.

groundnut and Jerusalem artichokes. The latter, a close relative to the sunflower, produces a potatolike tuber. Strawberries, raspberries, blackberries, and blueberries were gathered, and what wasn't eaten fresh was dried to provide fruit during the long winter.

The Narragansett, along with other Woodland tribes, learned the value of the sap of the maple tree and collected sap when it would run in late winter. To tap the trees, the Narragansett cut a large "Y" in the bark of a tree and then inserted a spile, or tap, made from the slippery elm. They then collected the sap in birchbark sap dishes.

In their fields, the Narragansett grew corn, beans, and squash as their main crops. Generally, women grew the crops and took care of the fields. One exception was that men tended small plots of tobacco, which was grown to be smoked during important ceremonies.

With corn as the main ingredient, the Narragansett made a number of dishes. Corn mush, also called *samp,* was crushed into a coarse grain and then boiled with currants until it became pastelike. It was either served plain or fried in animal fat. "Journey" cakes, or johnnycakes, as they were later called, were made of pounded, moistened cornmeal baked on a very long, narrow cake board made of red oak or other suitable wood and placed on the hearth stones. The Narragansett often carried these johnnycakes along with them wherever they went on long journeys.

They also parched and ground corn to be carried dry by hunters and other travelers. In this form, a Narragansett could carry enough corn for a forty-day trip in a small basket worn on the

In addition to what they hunted, the Narragansett grew a variety of foods.

back. For shorter trips, the parched cornmeal was carried in a belt pouch, and eaten hot or cold with a little water added to it.

Corn was also the main ingredient in a variety of stews. Stews would be made using corn, beans, squash, and whatever meat or fish was available. To thicken a stew, Narragansett cooks

This wooden bowl was used for cornmeal porridge.

*A Narragansett hunter
stalks a deer in the woods.*

added dried and powdered nuts, such as acorns, walnuts, and chestnuts. One special type of corn that the Narragansett grew is still a favorite treat today—popcorn.

The Narrangansett also made bean-hole beans. To do this, a pit was dug and lined with rocks, and then a fire built. When the fire died down the embers were removed, and a pot of well-soaked beans was placed in the pit and then covered. The heat from the rocks cooked the beans, which were often sweetened with maple syrup.

Fresh corn was either boiled or roasted, and then eaten on the cob. One way the Narragansett had of preparing roasted corn is still popular today as part of a clambake.

The Narragansett often held clam-bakes along the shores of the bay. A pit would have been dug and lined

Hunting and Fishing

The Narragansett were accomplished hunters. The major hunts occurred in the fall, after the crops had been harvested. The white-tailed deer was one of the most important animals to the Narragansett. Almost every part of a killed deer was used. The hide was turned into clothing and moccasins and cut into thin strips to lace things together. Antlers were used to make tools and arrowheads, and bones were fashioned into tools and ornaments. Sinews—the long tendons that connect muscles to bones—were the basis for thread, string, and bow strings. The meat was both eaten fresh and cut into strips and dried over a fire. The dried venison was eaten later, either alone or added to stews during the winter.

A variety of techniques were used to hunt deer. They might have been stalked and shot with bow and arrow,

with rocks, before a fire was built in it. As with the beans, when the fire died down, the ash and embers were removed before ears of corn in their husks were placed directly on the rocks and covered with a variety of shellfish. Lobsters were plentiful at the time and it was common for one to weigh over twenty pounds. The food was then covered with a thick layer of seaweed that held in the heat and helped season the cooking food. When the food was cooked, the seaweed was removed and all shared in the feast.

Narragansett fishermen cut holes in the ice in order to fish in the winter.

or caught in traps and snares that the Narragansett set. Communal drives were also organized, with as many as 200 to 300 people participating. For these drives, mile-long fences arranged in a funnel shape were built in the woods. The drivers would then start walking toward the fences. As the deer moved away from the drivers, they would enter the wide end of the funnel and then be driven to the waiting hunters. The hunters easily killed the deer as they were forced to pass through the narrow end of the funnel. Occasionally, the Narragansett hunters would kill a moose.

When the hunting party worked close to the village, women and children sometimes went along to help; but when the hunters went farther afield, the women and children remained in the village. Their hunting territory often overlapped with that of neighboring tribes, and conflicts sometimes arose.

In addition to deer and the occasional moose, the Narragansett hunters also killed a variety of small game. Waterfowl, which were very plentiful at the time, were shot with bow and arrow or sometimes netted. Swans, ducks, and geese were all part of the Narragansett diet. In the forest the hunters also killed turkeys and grouse.

The Narragansett also learned how to harvest the bounty of the waters that surrounded them. In the spring, temporary camps were set up along

Hand-woven bags and baskets were often used to store dried corn.

were attached to hand lines. They also built traps in some of the smaller rivers and streams, which forced the fish to swim through a narrow area where they could be easily speared or netted. In the summer, they fished the open waters of the bay and ocean from their dugout canoes. The first Europeans to visit the area reported that a Narragansett canoe was formed from just a single pine log and that the largest ones could hold as many as fifty paddlers. Much smaller dugouts were typical, however. In winter, when the Narragansett could not fish from shore, they cut openings in the ice of nearby ponds and fished through the holes.

Before the coming of the Europeans, the only domesticated animal that was found in a Narragansett village was the dog. Dogs were kept to help control the rodent population and serve as watchdogs to alert the village to strangers. Dogs were also a food of last resort when the village was short of meat. They were not kept as pets.

All cooked foods, other than those cooked in pits, were prepared over an open fire. The Narragansett made and used earthenware cooking pots in a variety of sizes. Bowls made of bark and wood were also used to prepare, store, and eat food. Food storage for the winter was extremely important to the survival of the group. Dried fish, shellfish, and meat could be hung in the dwellings. Corn, after it was dried, was put in large woven bags or baskets. Then a large pit was dug and a number of containers were buried together. Early European settlers learned of this practice and were known to have taken an entire village's winter corn supply.

rivers and streams where the runs of spawning fish could easily be harvested. The fish were quickly cleaned and then hung out in the sun to dry, or placed on a rack over a fire to be smoked. In addition to fish and eels, the Narragansett ate a wide variety of shellfish. Clams, scallops, oysters, lobsters, and crabs were all part of the catch. Women, primarily responsible for gathering shellfish, shucked the shellfish in teams. The raw clams, oysters, and scallops were skewered onto long green sticks and then dried and smoked. Lobsters and eels were preserved in the same way.

The Narragansett caught their fish with nets, as well as bone hooks that

Political and Social Organization

The main unit of the pre-European Narragansett was the village. Each village, which was made up of a few extended families, was led by a headman called a *sachem*. *Sachems* were most often men, although women were also known to have held this position. The position of *sachem* was often passed down from father to son, or daughter. The *sachem* made decisions with the consent of the people, and most often with the help of a council of elders. Together, they came to an agreement before the *sachem* made any decisions that affected the village. Each village had a specific territory, and any conflicts between Narragansett villages would be resolved by the *sachems*.

In times of war with neighboring groups, the warriors from a number of villages would band together. Most conflicts arose over claims for hunting territories. The style of warfare for all the Algonquian tribes involved what would today be termed guerrilla warfare. Groups would sneak about the forest ambushing parties from rival groups or making quick raids on their villages. Casualties were low, and warfare rarely upset the daily life of the people involved. Often, victories were more important for the honor gained by the winning side, rather than for any actual gains of territory.

The early European settlers of the area noted that the Narragansett held a position of power over some of their weaker neighbors. The Niantic, Massachusetts, Montauk, Pawtuxet, and other tribes owed allegiance to the Narragansett. These relationships may have existed before the coming of the Europeans, and were probably the result of a trade network that existed around the trading of *wampum*.

Wampum are strands of cylindrical shell beads strung together to form belts. The Narragansett and some of their neighbors were very skilled in crafting these beads, which were made from the thick center of a whelk shell and varied in color from white to purple. Dark quahog shells were often used for variety in the patterns. *Wampum* belts were highly prized by Native Americans to the north and west of the Narragansett. The early Europeans traded for *wampum* from the Narragansett in order to trade with other tribes for furs.

As European contact became more frequent and more demanding, the role of the *sachems* began to change. Europeans, who wanted to deal with as few people as possible, saw the *sachems* as the kings and queens of the Narragansett. It seemed the more control the Europeans exerted, the more powerful the *sachems* became. In response to this situation, soon only two *sachems* had control of all the lands of the Narragansett.

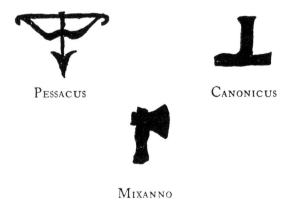

PESSACUS   CANONICUS

MIXANNO

Sachems used these marks to sign treaties in the 1600s. Their names are printed beneath the marks they used.

A Narragansett man and woman in traditional dress.

Clothing

Prior to the adoption of European materials and styles, the Narragansett men and women wore similar clothing. In the warm months, they wore a breechcloth and a pair of moccasins. The breechcloth was usually made from deerskin or sometimes sealskin. The moccasins were made from either deerskin or moose hide. Moose hide moccasins were preferred, because they lasted longer. Some moccasins were decorated with dyed porcupine quills and stiff moose hair. The decorated moccasins were saved for special occasions, while plain ones were worn for work and everyday wear.

A mantle, or cape, fastened over the shoulder was a useful garment. In the summer, it helped protect its wearer from the ever-present mosquitoes; in the winter, longer versions protected wearers from the cold. Mantles were made from a variety of materials. Woven mantles used the fibers of the hemp plant and grass. Ceremonial mantles were made of shimmering turkey feathers. Fur mantles were preferred in the winter for their added warmth. It took two deerskins or two bearskins to make a winter mantle that would reach the ground. A belt was often worn over the mantle to help secure it.

Leggings were also worn for protection from brush and brambles, as well as for warmth. The Narragansett used two different styles of leggings—a shorter version for women, which covered only the lower leg and was held up with garters; and longer ones for men, which came above the knee and were attached to their belts. Leggings of both styles had a strap that went under the foot and were often decorated in the same style as the moccasins.

Both men and women wore their hair long, usually pulled back in a ponytail or braid. Some of the men shaved their heads except for a strip left long down the center of their heads.

This brass hair ornament is believed to have been worn by a female sachem.

Games

Like many other Native Americans, the Narragansett played a game that the French called *lacrosse*. Two teams played on a 500-foot-long field. Players carried sticks with curved ends, to which woven, basketlike pouches were attached. A ball made of wood or deer hide was caught, carried, or thrown, using the pouch on the stick—never the hand. The object of the game was to throw the ball into the opponent's goal. When the Narragansett played *lacrosse,* one team would paint themselves white.

The Narragansett also played a game with a wooden disk. The disk was rolled across a field and the players ran alongside with eight-foot spears. The object of the game was to place a spear in the ground at the point where the disk was expected to stop. Once a game was started it often lasted all day.

A number of gambling games were also popular. In addition, young males of the village played at the skills of hunting and warfare that they would need once they reached manhood.

Narragansett men play a game of lacrosse.

A group of Narragansett celebrate the summer solstice.

Religious Life

Cauta'ntowwit was the god whom the Narragansett believed was responsible for their creation. When this god first attempted to make a man and woman out of stone, he was not pleased with the results. He destroyed his first attempts and tried again, using a tree as his raw material. *Cauta'ntowwit* was very pleased with this couple, and they became the ancestors of the Narragansett. *Cauta'ntowwit* also gave the Narragansett their first crops.

Believing that they had immortal souls, the Narragansett felt that after they died their soul would return to the land of *Cauta'ntowwit,* which was in the Southwest. The souls of thieves, liars, or other undesirables, however, would be excluded from the land of *Cauta'ntowwit* and forced to wander, lost among the known world.

In addition to this creator god, there were many other deities that were a part of the Narragansett religion. Roger Williams, the founder of the English colony in Rhode Island, made a list of thirty-eight of these lesser deities. Each Narrangansett member selected one of these deities as a personal god, or *manitto*, as the Narragansett called it. Often a person would choose a *manitto* after seeing it in a dream.

The Narragansett had a few major religious ceremonies at special times during the year. The winter and summer solstices, and the harvest, were three important celebrations. It was the harvest observation that the neighboring Wampanoags shared with the first Pilgrims—and is now celebrated as Thanksgiving. These ceremonies, and other religious occasions, were overseen by the religious leader, or *shaman*, of the village. The Narragansett called their *shamans powwows*, which is an Algonquian word that has come to mean a gathering of Native Americans.

In many ways, the role of the *powwow* was closer to that of a doctor than a priest. The Narragansett believed the *powwow* was able to call upon the spirits to help them cure illness.

A Narragansett was buried along with his or her most prized possessions. Men were buried with their weapons and tobacco pipes, as well as beads and *wampum* belts. Women were buried in their finest clothes, with their baskets and jewelry. It was believed that the souls of the dead would want these things when they reached the land of *Cauta'ntowwit*.

European Contact

It is estimated that in the early 1600s, the Narragansett had about 5,000 warriors. If that was the case, the total Narragansett population may have been between 25,000 and 30,000 people. In the late 1800s, the state of Rhode Island formed a commission to detribalize, or disband, the remaining Narragansett. At that time, they identified just over 300 Narragansett who were entitled to share in the money the state paid for the remaining Narragansett lands.

However, the worst enemies of the Narragansett were actually the diseases that arrived with the Europeans. Smallpox, measles, typhus, and other illnesses that many Europeans were able to survive usually proved to be fatal to Native Americans who did not have any immunities to them. In 1620, before the Pilgrims arrived in Plymouth, Massachusetts, a number of European explorers, traders, and fishermen had visited the coastal regions of the Northeast. In addition to metal knives, tomahawks, and glass beads, they brought disease.

One of the reasons that the Pilgrims did not find any immediate resistance to their colony was the fact that the native group that had lived in that area had been totally wiped out by diseases brought by the earlier European visitors. Epidemics ravaged the coastal region of the Northeast. In 1617, an epidemic of smallpox killed untold thousands of Native Americans who lived in the region. Exact information about the effects of these diseases is sketchy. We do know, however, that in 1633, 700 Narragansett died. We also know that in 1634, four Dutch traders who spent the winter with a group of Native Americans along the Connecticut River reported that of the 1,000 people who were living in the village in the fall, only 50 survived to see the spring.

Left alone, the Native Americans of the Northeast probably would have built up immunities to these diseases, and their population would have rebounded. But they were not given the opportunity. The Europeans upset the balanced life of the Native Americans.

The fur trade strongly encouraged Narragansett men to spend more and more time trapping, and less time hunting for food and helping with the farming. This would have been all right if the Narragansett had been able to trade the furs for food, but luxuries

The Pilgrims meet the Narragansett in 1622.

like cloth, beads, decorative metal items, and metal weapons were what they bartered for. Warfare among Native Americans increased and became more costly as they fought for territory using their newly acquired weapons. They also traded for alcohol, which created many problems for Native Americans.

The Narragansett who managed to survive the epidemics and war with neighboring tribes still had to confront the Europeans' lust for more land. At this time, there was no land in Europe

An illustration of the attack on the Pequots.

that was available for expansion. The Europeans who came to the Americas did so for a variety of reasons. Some came in search of fame and fortune, others came in search of religious freedom. Still others were forced to come as punishment for crimes committed in Europe. In North America, all who arrived saw that the wealth of the continent lay in its vast lands. The Native Americans, whose numbers were already declining due to disease, were seen as an obstacle to be overcome.

The first known European to visit the Narragansett was the explorer Giovanni da Verrazano in 1524, and for almost one hundred years European contact was limited to coastal traders. In 1622, the Narragansett had their first contact with the Pilgrims. Then, in 1636, the first Europeans settled in what was to become Rhode Island. Roger Williams, a Puritan who disagreed with the conservative leaders of the church, had left the Massachusetts Bay Colony to form a new settlement. When Williams and his followers arrived in the Narragansett lands, they were welcomed and sold land on which to settle. Williams's community was called Providence, which is now the capital of Rhode Island.

In the early years of European settlement in New England, the colonists were greatly outnumbered by the Native Americans. To counteract this, they allied themselves with some tribes and encouraged wars between Native American groups. In 1637, Roger Williams convinced his Narragansett neighbors to join with the Europeans in their war against the Pequots, who lived in what is today the state of Connecticut. The alliance of the Narragansett and Europeans, with the aid of European weapons, wiped out the entire Pequot group. Those who survived the fighting were divided up among the Europeans and the Narragansett to be used as slaves.

The Narragansett leader at the time was called Canonicus by the Europeans and Qunnoune among his own people. The Europeans, who tended to impose their own views and interpretations on new cultures, considered *sachems* to be the nobility of the Narragansett, and Canonicus the highest nobleman of the entire group. As the leader of the Narragansett, Canonicus counseled in favor of supporting the English in their fight against the traditional enemies of the Narragansett, the Pequots. Another tribe, the Mohegans, were also allied with the colonists in the Pequot War. After the Pequots were wiped out, conflicts arose between the Narragansett and the Mohegans.

The English settlers in Massachusetts and Connecticut formed what is called the United Colonies and continued their strategy of pitting one Native American group against another. The relations between the Narragansett and Mohegans had always been strained. After the Pequot War, hostilities between the two groups renewed. The leaders of the United Colonies forced both groups to agree to allow colonial leaders to settle differences between them. Canonicus had shared the leadership of the Narragansett with his nephew Miantonomi. In 1643, Miantonomi was captured in a raid on the village of the Mohegan leader, Uncas. According to the agreement with the colonists, Uncas turned Miantonomi over to them. But the

Marks used to sign papers by the sachem *Miantonomi, who was killed in 1643 by the Mohegans.*

colonial leaders decided to return Miantonomi to Uncas with secret instructions to execute him.

Uncas's brother, Wawequa, is believed to have been the Mohegan who finally executed Miantonomi in September 1643. Some historians believe that this treachery was a calculated attempt by the leaders of the United Colonies to cause problems for Roger Williams and his independent followers.

The crucial blow to the Narragansett was their participation in King Philip's War. King Philip, as he was called by the colonists, was the head *sachem* of the Wampanoags, and had tried to get along with his English neighbors. But in 1675, King Philip could no longer accept the intrusions of the colonists and led an uprising of the Native Americans of southern New England against the colonists. The Narragansett joined King Philip, while other groups still sided with the colonists. At first

King Philip's forces were successful and burned a number of outlying colonial settlements. Over one hundred colonists were killed in these raids. The colonists soon retaliated, however, and forced King Philip and his Narragansett allies to take refuge in a swamp near what is now South Kingston, Rhode Island. In the Battle of the Great Swamp, the Narragansett and other groups present were nearly wiped out. Those who survived the battle were driven into exile or captured. Many of the captives were shipped to the West Indies, where they were sold into slavery.

The colonists quickly occupied much of the land that had belonged to the Native Americans who had participated in King Philip's War. Once the war was over, the Niantics, allies of the Narragansett who had remained neutral, moved into southern Rhode Island and joined the few remaining Narragansett. This group was all that remained of the once-powerful Narragansett nation. Over the next one hundred years, these people and their descendants fought a losing battle to retain their identity as a people and to keep their remaining lands, located primarily in the area of Charlestown, Rhode Island.

In 1709, Ninegret II, the son of a Niantic *sachem,* gave up all claim to Narragansett lands except for sixty-four square miles in and around Charlestown. This deal also gave ultimate control of the Narragansett and their land to the Rhode Island legislature. In the ensuing years, the Rhode Island legislature was more likely to side with those trying to take more land away from the Narragansett rather than protecting Narragansett interests. During this time, the remaining Narragansett also intermarried with blacks and Europeans, making their identity as a tribe harder to prove.

The Narragansett Today

In 1880, the Rhode Island legislature passed a bill that nearly ended the existence of the Narragansett. This bill had the remaining Narragansett cede all their existing lands to the state and give up their claim to being a tribe. In exchange for this, the Narragansett received $5,000, which was divided among the 325 people that the state recognized as Narragansett. During the next one hundred years, many of the remaining tribe members stayed in the area of Charlestown, Rhode Island.

Fortunately for those who did remain, the Rhode Island legislature had violated the Indian Trade and Intercourse Act of 1790. This act had

been passed by the first U.S. Congress and signed into law by President George Washington. This law required federal approval of any transfer of Native American property, something the Rhode Island legislature had never done. In 1975, a suit was filed in federal court on behalf of the Narragansett. The result of this court case was that by 1983 the Narragansett were awarded public land and $3.2 million to purchase private land. This gave the Narragansett an 1,800-acre reservation in the Charlestown area. Another result of the court case was that the federal government officially recognized the tribe.

Anyone who could demonstrate that they had a relationship to one of the 325 people named in the 1880 detribalization settlement was considered a member of the newly recreated Narragansett tribe.

One problem that has faced the Narragansett since winning their case is division within the tribe. There appear to be two separate groups in Charlestown that have different ideas as to how the tribe should be managed. One is headquartered at the Charlestown Town Hall. The other group considers the Narragansett Longhouse, located on the reservation, to be its headquarters. Both claim to speak for all the Narragansett. The greatest disagreement between the groups concerns the question of gambling. Many reservations around the country have used their unique status as sovereign nations, answering only to the federal government, to set up gambling establishments that would be illegal if the reservation

The annual Narragansett powwow *in Charlestown, Rhode Island.*

were subject to state laws. Some tribes have found gambling a source of employment for their people, and of income for the tribe as a whole. Others have found the experience to bring more trouble than benefits. The state is opposed to it, but ultimately the Narragansett are once again in charge of their own fate.

Today, according to the 1990 U.S. Census, there are 2,456 Narragansett, 1,672 of whom live in Rhode Island. On their reservation in Rhode Island, the Narragansett host a number of festivals that demonstrate their Native American identity. The largest is the Narragansett Harvest Festival of Thanksgiving, which is held on the reservation in Charlestown each October. The Narragansett have created a housing authority that is trying to provide decent, low-cost housing for tribal members. In the 470 years since Giovanni da Verrazano first landed in Narragansett Bay, the Narragansett have managed to proudly hold onto their identity and heritage as Native Americans.

Chronology

1524   Giovanni da Verrazano visits the Narragansett.

1622   First Narragansett contact with the Pilgrims.

1633   Seven hundred Narragansett die in a smallpox epidemic.

1634   Four Dutch traders report that 950 Narragansett died during the winter.

1636   Roger Williams and his followers settle on lands purchased from the Narragansett.

1637   The Narragansett join the colonists in the Pequot War.

1643   The Narragansett *sachem* Miantonomi is captured by the Mohegan leader, Uncas, and later executed by Mohegans at the direction of the leaders of the United Colonies.

1675   King Philip's War begins, during which the Narragansett join the Wampanoags against the colonists.

1709   Ninigret II gives up claim to all but sixty-four square miles of Narragansett land and gives control of the tribe to the state of Rhode Island.

1790   The first U.S. Congress passes the Indian Trade and Intercourse Act, which requires federal approval of any transfer of Native American property.

1880   Rhode Island legislature passes a bill that pays the remaining Narragansett $5,000 to give up what is left of their lands and their status as a tribe.

1975   Suit is filed in federal court on behalf of the Narragansett to regain their land and tribal status.

1978   U.S. Congress passes a bill returning Narragansett land to the tribe.

1983   Federal government formally recognizes the Narragansett as a tribe.

INDEX

Acknowledgments and Photo Credits
Cover and all artwork by Richard Smolinski
Page 11: Courtesy of the Massachusetts Historical Society; p. 16: Haffenreffer Museum of
Anthropology, Brown University; pp. 17, 19, 28, 30: Courtesy of the Rhode Island
Historical Society; p. 26: The Bettmann Archive.
Map by Blackbirch Graphics, Inc.